T0147120

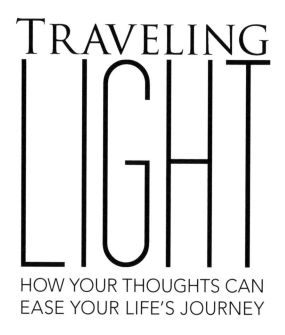

TRAVELING LIGHT

HOW YOUR THOUGHTS CAN EASE YOUR LIFE'S JOURNEY

Leonie van Hest

BALBOA.
PRESS

A DIVISION OF HAY HOUSE

Russell Hamlet Photography for the portraits.

Balboa Press books may be ordered through booksellers or by contacting:

Balboa Press
A Division of Hay House
1663 Liberty Drive
Bloomington, IN 47403
www.balboapress.com.au
1 (877) 407-4847

Because of the dynamic nature of the Internet, any web addresses or links contained in this book may have changed since publication and may no longer be valid. The views expressed in this work are solely those of the author and do not necessarily reflect the views of the publisher, and the publisher hereby disclaims any responsibility for them.

The author of this book does not dispense medical advice or prescribe the use of any technique as a form of treatment for physical, emotional, or medical problems without the advice of a physician, either directly or indirectly. The intent of the author is only to offer information of a general nature to help you in your quest for emotional and spiritual well-being. In the event you use any of the information in this book for yourself, which is your constitutional right, the author and the publisher assume no responsibility for your actions.

Any people depicted in stock imagery provided by Thinkstock are models, and such images are being used for illustrative purposes only.
Certain stock imagery © Thinkstock.

Print information available on the last page.

ISBN: 978-1-5043-0090-2 (sc)
ISBN: 978-1-5043-0091-9 (e)

Balboa Press rev. date: 01/11/2016

Contents

In her book "Traveling light", Leonie explains how we can teach ourselves to travel light on our life's journey, as long as we are able to shake off the negative thoughts and emotions like anger, envy, jealousy, worry or lack of self love...the baggage we have created for ourselves, that weigh us down.

Furthermore: Why not try to "*be*" that travelling light, wherever you go, shining like a beacon on the path of people who experience darkness or challenges in their lives and help them up, give them the hope that there is light at the end of a seemingly dark tunnel.

This book is dedicated to Neil,

My partner, soul mate and mentor...
With very special thanks for believing in me before I did...
For always encouraging and guiding me...
For allowing me to make mistakes, and by doing so,
helping me building up my confidence...
And most of all, for giving me space to find "me" again...
Thanks for always being right beside me!

PROFILE

Who is Leonie van Hest

Leonie was born and bred in Holland, where she started her working career at a boarding school for mentally disadvantaged girls. After she got married in her mid twenties, she and her husband travelled the world working in Holland, Saudi Arabia, South Africa, Namibia and 10 years ago they moved to New Zealand.

Their 4 daughters kept Leonie busy and she enjoyed her job as a stay at home mum for the first 10 years, before applying for the Administrator's job at a Day Care Centre on the west coast of South Africa.

For more than a decade she worked with 40 children between 6 months and 4 years of age.

Moving to New Zealand was the reason she resigned and because she is passionate about working with young children she started working as a nanny on Auckland's North Shore.

2 Years ago Leonie successfully completed a course in Holistic Counseling, meant to broaden her horizon on spiritual healing and help her understand herself better. She was so intrigued by the concept of positive thinking, especially about ourselves, that she felt the urge

to pass on her knowledge and started a practice named: "Heart of the Matter".

Her main aim as a healer, so she states, is to find the "heart" of what the "matter" is if some one needs her guidance. It is not her task to come up with answers for the mal-functioning or dis-eases in one's body but help her clients find the strength in themselves to discover where their "complaints" originate from and then subsequently heal their own body.

"Very often it is our own way of limited thinking and lack of self love that plays a major role in the blockages in our body, that prevent a healthy flow of energy and subsequently well being"

INTRODUCTION

Three years ago my husband suggested accepting an engineering job in a small village in the outback of Australia. I made the choice to stay behind and continue my life and work in New Zealand. The freedom that I felt and the realization that I could manage much better on my own than I anticipated, gave me the strength to finally, after 35 years of marriage, decide to distance myself from an unhealthy relationship. Throughout these years I had allowed myself to be controlled and had subsequently limited my ability to grow as a person. In my ignorance I thought pleasing and following my husband in order to make him happy was my main objective in life...What I really did was, I enabled myself (as well as my husband) to stay spiritually small instead of growing into my own happiness and purpose. In fact I didn't know what my purpose was... I had completely lost my direction and voice in this process due to feelings of inferiority, and misbelieve that I had nothing valuable to say.

Instinctively I knew I had to change this situation in order to look into my heart and follow my intuition. These years have felt like a rebirth for me...I felt I had been long enough in a protective environment where I was cared for, but at the same time tied to someone who made most decisions for me. It was time for me to try and stand on my own and learn from my mistakes in order to grow in confidence. In my marriage

I often felt treated like a child with my husband taking the role of my father, when what I wanted was to be acknowledged as an equal partner.

The road to find myself was difficult and sometimes painful.

In my family we have experienced this separation in different ways. My husband and youngest daughter are still coming to terms with it, but I have learned from my mistakes and my misunderstanding belief that I should please the people I love in order to make them happy... Our purpose in life I now believe is rather to be the best we can be and subsequently spread our talents of kindness, love, encouragement, understanding and wisdom and by doing so make a positive difference. How our kind actions are received or perceived though is beyond our control and the responsibility of the other party. No guilt should ever be instilled in the server if happiness is not the end result. I have to stress that again, since our purpose is only serving, not taking the responsibility for the other party's happiness.

In order to deal with my emotions of ***guilt*** for splitting up a family, ***fear*** for the future, ***hurt*** because I felt I had to end this relationship in order to find myself again, I intuitively felt it was the right thing to do. I started to read motivational books, listened to inspirational DVD's, enrolled myself for an on line course in Holistic Healing and started writing down, and analyzing every single feeling and emotion that was weighing me down.

It was at this time that I met my current partner Neil, and his at the time 6 year old son.

Neil was going through his own journey of hurt and frustrations as well as feeling emotionally, financially and physically drained.

But he wasn't bitter... He "introduced" me to the Secret, to Louise

Hay, Wayne Dyer, John Kehoe, Neal Walsh etc. But even more importantly: He expressed his belief in me! He believed I had a gift; a gift of always being positive and a gift to pass this positiveness on through words and a *yes* attitude. At that stage I wasn't so sure about that, mainly because I wasn't sure about my own strengths and potential and I hadn't grasped the concept yet that I wasn't responsible for anyone's happiness but mine.

I was hungry for the kind of information he offered me and read as much and often as I could. At times I was confused, because I did practice kindness, and encouragement and positive thinking already but over the past decades it was not always returned to me. Another revelation was the realization that it is not enough to act and talk positive only. The most important message that I learned was that I should be more loving towards myself! Believe in myself. Feel worthy. Find my inner strength and regain the power to stand up for myself. These qualities I possessed already but I had forgotten about them. It was easy for me to encourage others and see their strengths. I, on the other hand had allowed myself to believe the negative talk I was intimidated by.

Now I know that the way people treat you is not always what you deserve...some people are battling their own demons and are not capable of kindness or respect (yet). I say purposefully *"not yet"* because we all can learn to nurture our talents of love, kindness and forgiveness towards ourselves. All we have to do is take some time to practice these skills; a bad habit that has been practiced for years can't be changed overnight, but if you are willing to do this, your life will become more peaceful.

Another big revelation for me was the fact that our thoughts play a much bigger role in our well being than I could have imagined.

Repetitive negative thinking patterns can sooner or later create blockages in our energy flow that can manifest as dis-eases in our body.

The importance of positive thinking patterns should therefore not be underestimated.

Our body is a multi dimensional being, which means that our body, mind and soul are all inter related with one another.

Our body for instance needs nutritious food, exercise, and rest in order to be functioning well. A wrong diet could lead to overweight, a lack of ecercise could lead to stiffness and even depression and a lack of rest could lead to a burn out. If you ignore the needs of your body, your body will try to attract your attention by "talking" to you through its physical state.

What our soul needs in order to be healthy, are the things that make us feel good, joyful, excited and happy. It are those things that bring us fun, laughter and love; like watching funny movies, catching up with friends, walking in the surf, soaking up the sun or do a hobby that nourishes our soul.

And what our mind needs is a positive mental attitude and positive thoughts, about ourselves in the first place, but also about how we see the world.

Ignoring the needs of our soul and mind, can as much cause dis-eases in our body as ignoring the needs of our physical body can.

Positive thinking starts in the mind. These positive thoughts trigger how we feel and through our actions, we react to these feelings. Remember therefore to not only look after your physical body for it to function in a healthy way, but also to be kind to your mind and your spirit.

I thought I always had been a positive person but since I started focusing more consciously on the way I saw and thought about myself,

I realized that I, unconsciously, had created restrictions and boundaries for myself because of a fear of failing and a lack of self believe and self worth. For years I allowed myself to believe that I was inferior. That I wasn't smart enough to attend University, not computer literate enough to operate a PC or even cell-phone, too dumb to do my own banking, and too simple to change careers. Worst of all, I seriously believed every word my belief system was telling me.

In hind sight; all I did was continue to make an imprint on my subconscious mind that stated that I was not good or worthy enough... and I believed it. It might not have been true but in my mind it was.

If you repeat these statements in your mind, every day several times, year after year you believe them! You don't reflect and think about it... you *know* that you are not smart enough to attend University, or that the career you're in, is all you are capable of doing...

I realized that if you can create that negative belief system for yourself in your mind by repetitive negative self talk and believe it... you of course can also create a positive thinking/ belief system in your mind that tells you that you are great! That you are smart! That you will succeed! That you are a winner!

So repeat that as often as you can.

I was determined to change my thinking from talking myself down all the time to talking myself up. I consciously changed my thought pattern by putting positive thoughts in my mind. Over and over and over. I did it so often that it became a habit and now I do it automatically, leaving less and less space for negativity.

Don't underestimate the power of your thoughts. Thoughts are real forces.

Every thought is energy, and your mind can hear what you say. Therefore be alert about what you think.

Every action and experience is triggered by the energy of our thoughts and words, and by doing so we are starting the creation of our own reality. That is how the law of attraction works.

And yes...I finally did successfully finish an on line course in Holistic Counseling, I can manage my own banking business, I am confident enough to make my own decisions and I managed to write all my revelations down and bundled them in a book; primarily for my own healing, but soon to create awareness about the importance of our thoughts.

It dawned to me that my own repetitive negative thoughts had harmed me more than a possible enemy could have done...but the good news that I learned is, you can teach yourself to control your thinking pattern, talking to yourself in a way as if you are talking to your best friend.

All of our problems of fear, failure and doubts are because our mind is ruling us.

If you do let your mind take over, you allow yourself to be the slave and victim of your uncontrolled negative thoughts. It is as simple as that. We have to try and take control of our mind and our thoughts. Every day bit by bit...watch your thoughts...when a negative thought comes up...refuse to allow it to take root and grow bigger by changing the way you think.

By doing so you lay the foundation to build up a better and happier more peaceful "you".

Do you know that we all have the ability and power within us, to turn our lives into a more joyous journey?

Most important is to delete all thoughts of negativity as if you don't like yourself: Remove the words of self doubt, self criticism, fear, unworthiness, and replace them with positive ones.

Instead: Be full of encouragement, praise, forgiveness, kindness and love.

You'll find soon enough that when you start looking at yourself with more self love; negative feelings like anger, jealousy, revenge, bitterness, frustration etc. will begin to disappear at the same time. Because, when you are feeling good about yourself, there is no need to bring someone else down. Quite the opposite is true. In a good state of spirit you want to lift other people up; encourage them, believe in them, be a beacon of light in their life.

My new belief system has been a guide line for me to help me achieve a more relaxed, confident and "lighter" life.

The key has been repetition. And gradually your positive thoughts will outweigh your negative ones.

Therefore be aware of your thoughts and if they are negative, change them.

The following life lessons will help
you look at life differently!

"Think positive thoughts, especially about yourself"

The objective of positive thinking is not only to trigger positive energy but also to create positive action. Positive thinking, triggers positive feelings and subsequently positive actions. Positive thinking alone is not enough...Acknowledge your emotions and deal with the situations life is presenting to you.

Don't wait for things to get better before you start thinking positive...Positive people think positive first and then things get better. The Universe responds to what we give out.

Fundamentally there are no problems in the world...but we create them because of our worries and self doubt... Leave no room for negative and destructive self talk. Happiness starts with self love.

I remember a magazine article I once read about netball player Irene van Dijk in which she was interviewed and asked: "How do you feel about having to compete with girls 20 years your junior...?" She replied: "I'm eager for them to show me what they've got, cos I am pretty awesome!" That one answer said it all! That is *believing* in oneself and

thinking positive. Having *faith* in your own abilities and oozing ***power*** all at the same time.

How critical are you of yourself? Don't put limitations on your own abilities. How often does it happen that when you look back on things you have achieved you say: "Not in a million years did I think I could do that..." With every challenge you have to tackle...try to think; "I'll give it a try! Either I'll love it or I'll learn from it...Both ways it's the perfect choice" Think in terms of self love, of opportunities and ideas, of believe and greatness!

Reflect for a moment on how you like to see yourself and create a positive affirmation reinforcing that.

Say these positive affirmations several times a day that express just that, because you will become what you think...

The secret with affirmations is that you use the present tense: as if you have achieved it already. Not: "One day I will be fit and healthy" but "*I am* a fit and healthy thinking person" or: "I take pride in the work I do" or: "I am a strong and talented woman" or: "I am blessed in many ways" or "I am a great public speaker" or: "Today I am having a productive day" or one of my own favorites: "I am the kind of person.... who...(you can fill it in yourself) e.g....stays calm in stressful situations and solves all problems easily..." Choose an affirmation that you would like to see happen but say it as if you already have achieved it! Don't talk about the way you are...talk about the way you want to be.

You really have to repeat affirmations over and over and over. It is like making an imprint on your subconscious mind. If you repeat it often enough, your mind believes it as true. If you have heard your whole life from parents, or teachers or people in positions of authority (or even bullying kids at school), that you are dumb, or clumsy or too fat or too lazy or ugly or a word that kids like to use "too much of a loser..." to achieve certain goals or to be part of a group, then you start to believe that. Your ***belief system*** is created by what you believe! Not what is necessarily the truth...but what you believe is true...So if you hear it often enough, often, especially from a young age, you believe it and therefore, attract it. So if negative affirmations have a negative impact on you...so can positive affirmations have a positive impact on you.

So keep on repeating these positive affirmations through the day. Day after day. You start believing what you repeatedly hear! I am a great healer, I am a creative mind... I am a successful athlete... I am a smart thinker or I am at my perfect weight.

Or a Mantra that we all can use: "I am a winner!"

In order to achieve a constant state of well being and contentment we need to feel good about ourselves. ***Believe*** that we are good, beautiful, talented, amazing people. That is why, the very first step we need to take is: Feel good about ourselves!

And we can learn that. We can teach ourselves, by disciplining our thoughts!

Because the way we feel about ourselves is a result of how we think about ourselves.

If we can start giving ourselves the same praise, encouragement and recognition, we give our friends or kids, we are half way.

"Believe that you are amazing"

LIFE LESSON TWO

"Understand that you are responsible for your own happiness"

I t is not the circumstances in our life that causes our unhappiness; It's how we react/respond to those circumstances that determines our state of being. If we can take a step back when we are challenged and look at the situation as an observer, we give ourselves time to respond in a mature and positive manner.

It is important to have the power to stay in control of the situation and our emotions, instead of giving it away to other people by blaming them for our (unfortunate) position. Believe you are responsible for your own happiness and well being.

If we fully understand that concept and can implement that in our daily life, then we have made the next important step in the right direction to be a happier person.

The mistake most people make is that we like to blame circumstances or other people for everything that is not working in our lives. Not realizing that blaming others might be the most easiest way, but at the same time only effective for a short while because we are ignoring and not dealing with our own emotions. Emotions that will eventually surface again such as self pity, doubt, frustration, anger, insecurity, or loneliness. **Not** taking responsibility for our life or actions by blaming others, is giving **them** the power! Why do we do that then...Because it seems so much easier. We don't have to look at ourselves...and that suits lots of us because we don't always like what we see. I blame someone else...problem solved! But is your problem solved...or just coming back in a different jacket over and over again...?

We are 100 percent responsible for every experience in our life. Not for every situation but for the way we **experience** this situation...because our experience is created by the thoughts we think and the emotions we feel.

I give you a simple example: You are taking two of your friends on a relaxing day out, but after an hour the car breaks down. The thoughts you think now and the words you speak determine how you are experiencing the situation and therefore create a 100 percent responsibility for it. One might say: "That has to happen to me again" (Talking yourself down due to self pity) A second one might say: "Didn't you check the oil before we left" (blaming someone else) and a third one might say..." Good that I am an AA member. Who's for morning tea, while we wait for them to arrive..." Own the situation and take responsibility. What would your thoughts and words be...and which one do you think is in the better state of mind?

We all have the **ability** to **empower** ourselves in such a way that we **can** handle life's challenges more easily.

The empowerment that I am talking about is the inner strength to deal with all your challenges in a mature and natural way. Responsibility is the "ability" to "respond" in a mature manner. Remember that we have a choice. That we should look for the silver lining in every situation and think what **is** still positive right now. What can I still be grateful for instead of dwelling on what mis-fortune is happening to me again.

Teach yourself to change your thinking from blaming others or drowning in self pity, into owning the situation and repeat this lesson for yourself over and over again in order to get better and better at it, until thinking positive becomes something you do automatically!

If we say positive words often enough our subconscious mind accepts as truth whatever we like to believe...

That's why it's so important to talk positive about ourselves in the first place.

An affirmation or Mantra at the beginning of every day might help you and you can repeat it as often as necessary. It is like planting a seed; a starting point. Say it with as much feeling as you can.

It might be something like: "Today I am having a productive day" or "I am managing my time well" Think what would work for you!

Motivational speaker Robin Banks likes to apply the ABC rule as a reminder. Am I Accusing, Blaming or Criticizing someone else for the difficult situation I am in?

If your first response is to Accuse Blame or Critisize, it will leave you powerless! Doesn't matter who you blame...the weather, the government, your mother-in-law or the traffic...at that moment you have lost your power. But what if you translate it as Acceptance and Believe you have a Choice! Which response would leave you in power and subsequently in control?

Another misconception in our pursuit to happiness is that the accumulation of material things is the way to a more satisfied life. Remember that the concept of being happy is not in material things... They may be a blessing though, but they are all temporary. Being happy is a feeling, a state of inner peace, joy and harmony which you can create yourself by gratitude, sharing/giving, forgiveness and focusing on what you have instead of on what's missing. Therefore try to restrict yourself on thoughts like: "I'll be happy if....." "I'll be happy if he marries me....." "I'll be happy if I get a raise..." "If I have my own house…" "If I lose 10 kg..." Instead focus on the 1001 blessings that you are showered with every single day and feel the abundance that surrounds you. Train your brain to think in *love* for what you *have* instead of focusing on what you *don't have*. Your partner, your job, your house, are all blessings but at the same time also temporary because you have no control over them. That's why we need to express gratitude on a daily basis for all these things and at the same time realize that the things that make us happy are the things we cannot touch or hold.

Don't let your happiness depend on things you have no control over.

"Don't give your power away by blaming others"

"Don't allow other people or outer circumstances to affect your good mood or joyful day"

S tart every day with a Mantra or positive affirmation: something like: "Nothing and no one is going to spoil this beautiful day for me today. I am in charge of how this day is going for me and that will be awesome!"

We have an enormous amount of power and love within us that helps us to be in charge of how we feel. Never give that power to anyone else by letting their behaviour, hurt your feelings of security and happiness.

We all know how it feels when we start the day and all goes well until a colleague spoils our mood with a nasty comment, or our kids walk over a just mopped floor or you need to be somewhere in time and there's a slow driver in front of you or your partner forgot your birthday... again....all reasons for us to lose our cool! We, again, by loosing it, give our power away to outer conditions that we have absolutely no control over. What we have control over though is our reaction to it.

You might say; "yes but...so and so knows exactly how to push my buttons and he makes me so angry that I lose it sometimes..." I agree. I know what you mean, but if you lose it, you have at that very moment put your power in the hands of the other party. The other party uses this power to bring you down. Sometimes consciously as if it is their mission in life to make you feel miserable, but sometimes unintentionally.

Whatever the reason for their behavior is, stay calm and collected and if you can but this is a major challenge...stay charming. Stay centred inwardly and know that none of this behavior is about you.

No one should take away your joy or rain on your parade by trying to strip you of your good feelings. Don't allow that to happen. Keep control over the situation and people will leave you, alone. They will look for someone else to over-power.

Someone who is showing abusive behavior like shouting or installing anger or guilt in you is possibly more uneasy with himself than with you. This is not to condone poor behavior but for our own spiritual growth we must be aware of their pain. Reflect for a moment, let the feeling of frustration or hurt or anger subside and let it go, allowing yourself not to let their outbursts or rudeness affect your good mood.

When in a constant state of feeling good, there is no need to bring some one else down through anger or abusive language. Furthermore, there is no need to give some one else permission to bring your mood down by an abusive attitude.

If you feel good (or if you want: feel "God") you want to spread this positive energy with everyone around you plus you can more easily look for the positive in others and point these strengths out. If not...you are more likely to look for flaws in others and highlight them, in order to feel better about ourself!

If we are in a situation though where people keep on bullying/hurting us repeatedly with their words and actions, move on! No one has to keep up with continuous disrespect! If that is difficult for you, ask yourself why you think so little of yourself that you allow people to keep on hurting you. Don't try to get even but love yourself and let go!

Hurt, brought onto you, is a very strong emotion, but although you may feel hurt try not to be angry...

You may feel hurt, but don't practice jealousy...

You may feel hurt, but don't waste your time taking revenge...

Anger, jealousy, and revenge are all toxic negative emotions that weigh you down!

Allow yourself to feel hurt or frustrated but demonstrate forgiveness...

Allow yourself to feel hurt or frustrated but demonstrate understanding...

Allow yourself to feel hurt or frustrated but demonstrate self love and kindness....

Try to feel compassion for the one who is hurting you, because that person is possibly walking a challenging path...Someone who loves oneself has no need to hurt another.

That won't be easy always but if you can, you will experience a calmness coming over you that brings peace of mind.

Hurtful feelings need to be digested before they can slowly subside.

It might happen that you can't sleep because a mean comment from a friend keeps on popping up in your mind...or you are overwhelmed by feelings of self doubt again. I am sure you can come up with your own example...You are not repeating the negative words 5 times but 500 times and you don't know how to stop it! Believe me, it happens to me too sometimes...I calmly try to digest the upsetting words or actions and keep on repeating that I am hurt but don't want to take revenge. That I am hurt but try to understand where it came from. That I am hurt but know at the same time that it is not about me. That I am hurt but that whatever the challenge is, love is the answer.

If things get out of hand and I have been lying awake for hours, I visualize stuffing all these feelings of disappointment, or worry, self doubt, even guilt, or sometimes anger about things beyond my control, into the pockets of my jacket, then I hang this jacket on a tree or anywhere where I am not reminded of my sorrows and feel suddenly **lighter.**

As if these negative feelings or the jacket, have literally weighed me down and are now swapped for feelings of liberation, inner strength and self belief.

I then visualize going for a swim in the ocean, or a walk in the forest, or just meditating in a beautiful garden. As long as it'll bring solace for me.

Don't try to get even with who or what caused you pain, but love yourself and move on. Let go!

In his book "Long walk to freedom" Nelson Mandela states: "As I walked out of the prison on Robben Island, where I was held captive for 27 years as a political prisoner my thoughts were: I am now walking out the door towards my freedom, and I know that if I don't leave all the anger, hatred and bitterness behind, I am still in prison"

Free yourself from negative thoughts and energy brought onto you by people and situations you have no control over, and look for the things in life that make your heart sing instead of sink.

**"Look for the positive in others
and you will find it"**

LIFE LESSON FOUR

"Don't listen to the well meant advice of other people telling you how to live your life or which choices to make"

Other people might not necessarily understand your life and that is OK because they don't have to live it.

Maybe if they could walk a mile in your shoes they might have an idea but do what feels good to you.

Wayne Dyer says it so clearly: "When your intuition, your gut feeling, your spiritual heart all know beyond any doubt, what to do, then don't be swayed by the fear based arguments of others. Sometimes meaning well and sometimes not...They might lead you astray from your joy.

The real objective of life is to grow, learn, and consistently align yourself to living in peace, harmony, and freedom"

With trying to fit into our (sick) society by behaving the way that others expect from us and by wanting and accumulating more and more stuff, we are keeping up a struggle. We should try and stop worrying about what other people think about us, only then can we experience joy and inner peace and that is what should be our ultimate goal.

Most important is that *you* know what you want to do or where you want to go and you only listen to your own words. Follow your intuition.

Train yourself to ignore the advice of other people that is maybe well meant but often a result of ignorance and a lack of understanding. Keep on focussing on the plan that you have set out for yourself, rather than follow the advice of others in order to please them. At the end of the day the only person you have to answer to is "*you*"

"Constantly align yourself with the Source in order to create harmony in your life"

"Know the difference between power over and power within"

I couldn't agree more with Susan Jeffers, in her book: "Feel the Fear and Do It Anyway" where she states the following:

"Power within means power over your perception of the world, power over how you react to situations in your life, power to do what is necessary for your own self worth and self growth, power to create joy and satisfaction in your life, power to act and power to love.

This power has nothing to do with anyone else. It is not ego centred but a healthy self love. It leaves us feeling free, since you are taking charge of your own actions and don't expect anyone else to do it for you. It is not the ability to get someone else to do what you want them to do. It is the ability to get yourself to do what you want to do. Own that kind of power...otherwise you lose your sense of peace and find yourself in a very vulnerable state of being."

Some people think that they have power because they have power **over** other people. That is not the personal power I am talking about. In fact having power over other people is just the opposite. In order to feel power, those people control other people to feel powerful. The reaction of fear, anger, frustration and hurt they get in return to their controlling nature makes them feel on top of the world. But the reaction of the controlled person might change… Instead of reacting frustrated, they might one day decide to let all frustration go and accept the situation without giving the overpowering person the pleasure of their upset state of mind. Hurt might turn into humbleness…and suddenly those people will lose their feeling of power. Because it's a fake power! The ability to tower over other people depends on the control they have **over** people and situations of the outside world instead of inner strength and personal power.

Remember that we are in control of our own happiness as long as we keep power over our own actions. It's not necessary to attempt to control others…their happiness is their responsibility. Dr. Wayne Dyer states: "Rather try to create growth in others by believing and encouraging them without dominating or ruling"

If you feel the need to control others…let go. You might be pleasantly surprised how capable your kids, friends or employees are without your interference…

"Demonstrate self love through self acceptance and self appreciation"

LIFE LESSON SIX

"Let your motive be "love" in everything you do"

Try to let "love" be the main motive for everything you do.

Not fear, guilt, or personal approval...in the long run it's not going to make your life easier.

If fear, guilt, revenge, anger, greed or any other negative emotion is consistently the main motive for your actions you are slowly poisoning your mind, soul and possibly your body.

Only love is the healing power in all your challenges.

Only love dissolves anger.

Only love gets rid of guilt.

Only love fades away fear.

Love for ourselves is the power that heals us.

Remember that good thoughts trigger good emotions and subsequently good actions. The opposite is also true! Stay away from negativity. Your body will love you for it.

Buddhism defines it beautifully...stating that "Loving someone is willing or wanting the happiness of another, and that is when you yourself experience the highest happiness. That is real love"

Wanting that happiness for another can be through serving and listening to your loved one's problems, resisting the temptation to give solutions. Practice unconditional love by giving them the space to do what nourishes their soul. This might not be what you want them to do but unconditional love has no conditions. Think about this definition when your motive has strayed...

At the same time remember that your aim and end result would be the happiness of the other through your kindness, love, encouragement, and support, but if this state of inner peace is not achieved by your loved one, you can't be held responsible for this. Everyone is responsible for their own happiness.

And the same counts for you. You should be loved for the person you are and given the space to do the things that make you happy and let you grow as a person.

Remember that you are amazing the way you are. You are precious. See yourself as a diamond: unique and beautiful. The people who recognise you as such will treasure you, admire you, and treat you accordingly.

Don't allow other people to try to change you to their liking... You should be loved for who you are. Stay true to yourself. You will lose your shine if you allow others to change you...A person who wants to see beauty in you will find it over and over again. One who can't find the beauty in you, possibly can't find the beauty in himself either.

"Whatever the question...
Love is the answer"

"Be grateful and content for what life is offering you instead of focusing on what's missing"

Happiness is not created by all the material things we have accumulated but it's reaching an inner peace through gratitude and contentment for what life offers us.

Thinking of what is missing in your life and always striving for more, overlooking all the blessings that you are showered with, is not a good base for inner peace and happiness. Think more and more good thoughts of gratitude and soon they will come automatically. Once it becomes normal, on a subconscious level again, you start attracting good things to you. The happiness of your life really depends on the quality of your thoughts; That's why you should make sure that your thinking is positive!

Never let a day pass without looking for the good around you, praising what you have and feeling blessed and grateful.

If we constantly focus on what we don't have, we mentally impoverish ourselves.

As important is to embrace change! Your life might change from one day to another. You might be in the unfortunate position to lose your job, a partner, a certain life style, or your health...If you can turn this negative situation into something positive by saying : "How can I let this set back work for me in stead of against me" then you are on the right track! Then you are not only accepting change, you are embracing it! This could be the ideal time to start something you had always wanted to do...or look at life with more appreciation, and subsequently find more inner peace. It's so important to stay grateful because everything you send out into the Universe comes back to you. If you send gratitude into the Universe, the Universe will send more things back to you to be grateful for. If you send discontent or constant criticism into the atmosphere it comes back with more "crap"

Address and acknowledge your feelings of sadness or frustration though, but try not to dwell on them too long. Instead look for the silver lining in the new situation. There will be one!

A remarkable quote from the Indian poet Kabir states; "The fish in the water that is thirsty needs serious professional counselling"

And so do we: We live in a world of abundance...The ones who cannot see the blessings and beauty that surrounds us and are wanting more or having the feeling of not ever having enough are in need of help!

"Be grateful for the abundance of blessings you are showered with daily"

"Get into a habit of making a positive difference in someone else's life by believing in them"

I often think, where would I have been now, if I hadn't met Neil... If I didn't had a number 1 fan who believed in me before I did...Who reached out and helped me to get my confidence back, who didn't judge and didn't criticise, but was patient and oozed an inner knowing that all would be good in the end.

I know that we shouldn't listen to negative talk from others...and be strong, thinking and talking positively to ourselves as if we are talking to our friends, but sometimes if we are not strong or sure enough we need that beacon of light to guide us in the right direction...To let us feel that we can do it...To help us up or point out our strengths that we are not yet able to see ourselves. To ensure us that underneath all our insecurities is an amazing person who is eager to get out of that prison, created by ourselves and who is determined to follow her/his heart and fly.

Be aware of the people around you that need your encouragement and inspiring words.

You might be that person who changes their life forever...Just by being your beautiful self and practicing a deed of kindness, understanding, support, wisdom, or forgiveness.

People most in need of support and help are often insecure or struggling with self acceptance.

There are also people who tend to push others away with their angry, hostile or over powering attitude... Pick up your courage and try saying something nice to them too. Uplift their spirit. I don't mean that you should become immediately best buddies...Just express acknowledgement to them that life is tough and difficult sometimes but that you admire them for their knowledge, their dress sense, their way with words; if you are willing to lift them up you will find something to praise them for, giving them a chance to look at themselves with different, more positive eyes. With your kindness you are planting a little seed that has the possibility to grow! Sometimes that's all a person needs…a start, a helping hand, a kind word, an acknowledgement or encouragement that helps them move forward and believe in themselves more.

People everywhere around you are hungry for that approval for someone to speak positive, encouraging and loving words about their life.

Pastor Joel Osteen, believes we can make a difference by creating wholeness, not destructiveness. He states;

"Encourage someone who's struggling with low self esteem, or feels down or depressed.

Talk faith into them when they think they cannot do it themselves. Support them in achieving their goal.

Be that number 1 fan in someone else' life: Say: "I believe in you!" "You've got what it takes!" or "I am behind you one hundred percent!"

You are a winner.

I am so proud of you.

I think you will do great things..."

Are you believing in anyone?

What kind of difference are you making in your child's life, in your partner's life, your friends' life...?

Are you making someone's life better because you have taken the time to listen to their goals and dreams and have expressed belief and faith in them?

You may be that positive person in someone else's life: Encourage them to not give up, lift their spirit when they seem discouraged and have strayed from their purpose. Be happy with them when they celebrate a milestone or achievement, say a prayer when they are struggling, and encourage them to let their mistakes be a lesson to get **better "at"** life! Not **bitter!**

You are making a difference in the life of another more than you can imagine!

Believe it or not but our purpose on earth is not to get lost in the dark but to be a beacon of light so that others may find their way! Let your actions inspire others! Let your light shine wherever you go!

**"Giving is a gift to others as well
as to yourselves"**

LIFE LESSON NINE

"Let your life be led by faith instead of fear"

Follow your intuition and have faith that it will lead you towards your purpose in life and will be for your well being and the well being of the people you meet.

Being free from fear and doubt, will bring you a great feeling of relief, of lightness that can lift you up.

Sometimes things don't make sense right now but believe and have faith that in the bigger scheme of things all will be clear and that time, will bring clarity.

Don't let fear lead your life! Believe that everything happens for a reason. Have faith that everything that comes to you in life is designed to make you a master in your positive talents. Even challenging times or people are a gift. It's a chance to practice humbleness, patience, love, kindness, understanding, forgiveness or wisdom. Have faith that all happens in the right time, with the right people in the right order.

Trust the process. Have faith that you are exactly where you are meant to be. Remember that behind every cloud there is definitely a bright shining sun! Trust that all clouds/challenges will eventually reveal a brightness. Be open to all the abundance the Universe has to offer you.

"Relax...nothing is under control"

LIFE LESSON TEN

"Let go of control"

Most of our frustrations in life occur, when we unsuccessfully want to control things we cannot. This is a habit that is based on fear...As if things will all work out as long as that you have control over them. But most of what life has presented to us, we have no control over...Find peace and inner calm by letting go of control. Have faith that all will be good in the end, even if things don't happen as fast or exactly the way you want to.

Letting go of control is letting go of worry, off stress and fear, welcoming inner peace, harmony, contentment and acceptance. Live in harmony in alignment with the Source, with Love, with your Higher Consciousness, with God, the Creator or any other terminology that feels comfortable for you. You then free yourself from control and live in harmony with the source you originated from.

Think, feel and visualise yourself as healthy and being protected from danger. A positive affirmation or Mantra that can help you to release worry and stress could be: "I am always protected from danger" or "I live in harmony with all that is love" I trust my intuition to guide me" and gradually your limiting feelings of stress, control, fear and worry will disappear and positive uplifting feelings of peace, acceptance, and inner strength will surface.

You will slowly become what you think!

You will attract what you feel

And you will create what you visualise.

"Let your intuition be your guide"

"All the above is within your grasp"

A s long as you believe in yourself!
Your beliefs and self talk are a very powerful energy. They can either lift you up or bring you down, depending on the quality of your thoughts. And still most of us are not living in this desirable peaceful state of mind and body...

It comes down to disciplining your thoughts and that needs repetition and consistency. Not only when you think about it but preferably consciously taking time out every day to say thank you for all the blessings and abundance in your life, to pay gratitude, Say a little prayer for someone in need, stay open to the silver lining in every situation, say your positive affirmations especially about yourself, create a Mantra for the day, to mentally send someone love or kindness. Keep on looking at life and the people around you through the eyes of God.

Be aware of your thinking and don't dwell on negative thoughts... delete these thoughts and change them into positive ones. If it's difficult for you to physically take 10min out every morning or night, practice positive thoughts while you are waiting at traffic lights, standing in the queue at the shop, waiting in the waiting room at the doctor's or when you cannot sleep...Soon you will begin looking forward to it too, because it'll make you feel good. It'll make you feel God.

Remember that thoughts are energy. That's why it's important to keep them positive...! Positive thoughts and feelings give you energy. Negative thoughts on the other hand will drain you.

So go ahead. Your body, mind and soul will love you for it. I promise!

"What are you waiting for...?"

ACKNOWLEDGEMENTS

A very special thanks to the following people, whose words of wisdom or quotes are being used to reinforce my philosophy and belief system.

Susan Jeffers, Ph.D. www.susanjeffers.com to learn more about Susan and her work.

Dr. Wayne Dyer

Robin Banks

Nelson Mandela

Irene van Dyk

Joel Osteen

Kabir

Printed in the United States
By Bookmasters